Options Trading

Options Trading 1 and The Predictable Stock Trading System

By: Sam Sutton and Stephen Smith

Options Trading for Beginners

Subtitle: A Beginner Guide to Start Making A Ludicrous Amount of Money with Options Trading

By: Sam Sutton

Table of Contents

The Predictable Stock Trading System

Introduction

What Is Options Trading?

The stock market might look like a terrifying earth to people, for first taking their step in the stock exchange. However, people can see, there are variations of securities depositors, and the people need for their removal. There is like security, identified as a choice to release the entrance to the world of prospects for investors. The option is an agreement which delivers a customer the accurate, but on the other hand, they do not offer the duty to purchase and sell a significant advantage at an exact value otherwise earlier an assured date. These purposes are taken as a compulsory agreement through correctly cleared terms and features. The option is just like a bond which is safe. An option is also a deal that is severely well-defined with conditions and assets.

Now, the question in your mind is what the variance between the options and stocks is? Well, the stocks will offer you a minor portion of proprietorship; on the other hand, options is an agreement which will provide you the rights to purchase or trade the stock at an exact price by an exact date.

An options trading was innate in 1973, so that once an options market developed to a dynamic marketplace. As said by statistics amassed by the Options Industry Council, the entire capacity of option agreements operated on the U.S. exchanges in 2007 was about 3 billion, and it was a record.

The market has subsequently developed through to a classy exchange vehicle. For example, you could predict; several market consultants also some depositors who formed plans and which are known as options trading tactics. The first supposed option purchaser was the Greek mathematician and theorist Thales of Miletus.

For several persons used to through exchange stocks, it might be correct that they are excited to response to the requests. So, what are the options trading? It is the common question for the people. The most important answer of it is that it operated options or choice that always worth your privileges on the stock market. It means a single person takes the rights to the marketplace or else buying individual stock ensuring a particular period and amount range. A call option is that the buyer decides in purchasing securities, though at the time marketing securities and it known as the put option. Therefore, in several circumstances, when other customers apply both of these choices including the similar stock, that keep an eye on the specified date and amount value. It is mostly known as the dual option transaction.

I am sure; you need to know a lot about options trading. If you want to, then you should be aware of the term. Possibly the toughest portion is that how to identify the different conditions. When you catch the opportunity to know this guff which they procedure to change schemes, it would be stress-free to create choices. It permits you to consider directly about the worth of the stocks, uncertainty there are actions to guess. You can choose well on whatever exchange options to the procedure when your information of this particular scheme is sufficient. A wise sample is, once the price of the stock rises, the best choice is to think through a call option. The benefit of it, you will be able to buy the stock at the poorer price as well as sell the stock at the above price in future.

Though this hint is workings, if the price of the stock rises and if not, you can discover it tough to the market. The stocks since they converted unworkable. Once you select the transaction option, you only purchase the stocks and after their actual worth go down. It is a reverse way of a call option. Each of the two options, you need the chance or correct to recompense a quality to the seller. It is while consuming particular exchange methods to obtain the place and stay capable of making benefit.

Option cash is the most skilled dealers demand the fraction; you are giving. It is real, whatever you may lose in the event the stock market changes differing your tactics. Options trading develop beneficial on this condition since you need restriction even uncertainty you're wasting money. For the reason of this, several brokers deliberate the trade options since if you're scared of devoting new funds for your schemes, you need to be coincidental to think through capitalizing slight amount. It simply worth that, you need to acquire to trial once uncertainty you need to use the options trading over get knowledge about the strict policies. If you are self-assured sufficient to follow your plans, this is vital to choose precisely to escape compelling yourself. Currently, you may also learn about the changed expensive exchange software through online. It can also give you advantages to spread your goals.

The benefit of Options is:

1. Better Price Competence

2. A smaller amount of Danger (depend on how purchasers use them)

3. Higher Possibilities of Earnings

4. More Tactical Replacements

There are several kinds of stuff to think while sharing options:

1. You are not beholden to take an action through the options which you are buying. For a wise example, when you are buying options and decide not to do anything through them the options convert valueless when the finishing date of 30 days to some years passes. However, you could misplace hundred percent of your venture in the choice at that idea.

2. Options are usually agreements on the stock otherwise an index and in most circumstances, be contingent on which is the primary advantage of an option. The brokers of the options don't hand over

several properties, till the purchaser agrees to go to the options which they have bought.

3. By learning the specific stocks, you are thoughtful of chasing the option on; however, you can relief yourself by escaping damages and valueless options at a period of finishing.

There are also two simple types of options usually available, and they're:

1. The call option is, once a buyer purchases the privileges to an approved upon the amount of an original stock or another benefit from the broker. These usually bought, when the purchaser assumes the stock to increase in worth. It is mandatory for the buyer to take steps on these types of options earlier the choice finishes if it creates economic logic to make sure of consequently.

2. The put option is often the opposite of a call option. In that case, the put option purchaser has a right to vend an advantage at a prearranged value, earlier to the termination of any put options. So, these could usually be bought uncertainty the buyer imagines the stock or another benefit to dropping the price.

There are almost four kinds of members in the options market. It depends on the position the member usually take. The positions are-

1. Purchaser of Calls

2. Brokers of Calls

3. Buyers of Puts

4. Brokers of Puts

Those people who purchase options are known as holders, and those who trade options are known as writers. Moreover, purchasers of calls and puts are assumed to have long positions, but the brokers of calls and puts are considered to have short positions.

There is some essential difference between purchasers and brokers of call and put options. The differences are-

1. Call holders and put holders known as purchasers are not indebted to purchase or vend, they only have the choice to use their rights if they decide to use.

2. Call writers and put writers known as brokers are indebted to purchase or trade. The brokers might be needed to create decent on an undertaken to purchase or trade.

Options exchange may contain a good agreement of danger, after you bought separately, however, if you are well-informed and if you can take classy steps that create the usage of options not as much of dangerous and more satisfying than unpretentious stock obtaining. If the depositor creates the strength required to edify themselves on these following techniques, then they can drive a long way to make a decent salary and reducing their danger.

Did you know that a large percent of people who make a lot of money lose it within the first couple years?

It doesn't take much for a person to lose all of their money. Around 2 in 3 lottery winners lose all of their winnings within 5 years. If someone could lose hundreds of millions of dollars over a couple years, how fast will you lose your millions that you could make from this book?

Over the past couple years I have stumbled upon the key secret behind managing money and KEEPING it. If you follow the link below you will uncover the truth behind managing and keeping the money you make

>>> Click/Tap here to Learn the Secret Behind Money Management

<<<

Chapter 1: Learning the lingo

An option trader is anybody that purchases as well as offers choices within the capital marketplace. A good investor is actually anybody that purchases as well as offers choices within the capital marketplace. Because trading options are most often carried out via on the internet buying and selling agents. It is also often called on the internet trading options or even on the internet choice buying and selling.

Before starting your service as option traders, you will have to know the lingo.

What is lingo?

This is accurate within just about any stroll associated with existence. However, it's especially accurate with regards to buying and selling choices. Along with choices, a few people are associated with conditions to comprehend. A few of these conditions, such as places as well as phone calls, are extremely fundamental and you ought to know about all of them.

A few conditions, nevertheless, need a bit more description. Whenever putting a good choices purchase, you need to be sure that you obtain the text properly. The next "language" can make much more feeling while you have more acquainted with choices. Because choices tend to be therefore flexible as well as because you may be each a choice purchaser as well as a choice vendor, it's essential that you should understand the next conditions:

Fundamental Trading options Conditions

Purchasing to Open -- When you wish to purchase over the phone or perhaps a place choice, you'll be buying phone calls to open or even buying places to open up. You're the purchaser, and also you tend to be buying to open a brand new placement.

Promoting to Near -- Let's state you purchase the phone choice with regard to $3. Throughout the following fourteen days, this rises within worth in order to $5. Therefore, you choose to market your own phone choice (this had been the buy to open). When you wish to market, the actual lingo is selling to near. You purchased something to begin a situation; you're promoting this in order to near away which placement.

Promoting to Open up -- You are able to open up a situation through promoting a choice. Think about this as the choice author or even alongside it from the agreement that's heading to defend me against a good responsibility. In the event that you will create the protected phone, for example, you'd currently personal the actual share. However, to complete your own choice purchase, the actual expression is selling phone calls to open (followed through regardless of the 30 days as well as hit cost may be). In order to open up this particular placement, you're promoting as well as consuming the actual high quality.

Purchasing to Near -- When you attend near away your own protected phone placement, you need to near the actual deal through purchasing back again that which you offered. Therefore, the buy is to close the purchase.

Marketplace Vs Restrict Purchases

The main kinds of purchases (for each share as well as options) tend to be marketplace or even restrict purchases.

The market order indicates a person is prepared to purchase the protection from its presently detailed cost. This is unable to imply your assured cost. Costs can alter, however, usually purchases undergo rapidly that you'll most likely end up receiving the detailed "ask" cost (if you're purchasing, which is). Unless of course, the fundamental share is shifting quickly (thus producing all of the choices relocate lock-step), you'll be stuffed possibly from or even correct around the detailed "ask" or even "offer" cost.

The "limit purchase," however, is exactly where a person state what cost you need to purchase the choice with regard to (or market the possibility with regard to should you currently personal it).

Why make use of restrict purchases? Nicely, for just one, they're excellent resources to make use of whenever you can't hold off your PC the whole day awaiting the best cost to look. Obviously, if you wish to purchase something for any better cost compared to happen to be detailed, you aren't assured of purchasing within from which cost. However because of share cost variances throughout the day, it's incredible the number of occasions you are able to sneak within in a somewhat much better cost, simply because of the choices encounter every single day.

Day as well as GTC Purchases

Just like shares, you have to state a period component for every purchase. Both of the typical purchases tend to be "day orders" and also "good 'til canceled" (GTC) purchases. Along with each purchase, you'll more often than not key in the "day" purchase. In the event that you're prepared to purchase at this time, a person may state each day purchase (then hang in there to ensure you're stuffed upon which trade).

It's not really enjoyable to understand per week later on that you simply in no way purchased within the industry a person believed a person do (especially when the share or even choice is actually upward substantially), therefore it's better to key in day purchases whenever creating jobs.

Halts

An end purchase is definitely a purchase which will get into impact whenever a particular cost is arrived at. This particular seems as being a restricted purchase. It stops the position beneath where the share or even choice happens to be buying and selling.

For instance, you have 10 agreements associated with XYZ Corp. You purchased all of them with regard to $3. forty (or $3, 400). You need to walk out a city, as well as in case XYZ doesn't proceed the proper way (up), you need to bend from this industry in a particular cost as well as restrict your own deficits. This is actually the ideal scenario with regard to putting an end purchase.

Keep in mind, whenever purchasing choices have the built-in cease associated with types. (Therefore you are able to just shed the limited, restricted amount of cash -- how much money this required to purchase the possibility, to begin with. That's the most you are able to shed, and that's why it's a kind of the "stop" purchase.)

However more to the point, if you choose to key in an end purchase that's as well near to the present bid/offer on the specific choice. You could discover yourself halted from the industry sooner than you anticipate (maybe because of a good intra-day slip associated with a few kind). As well as even worse, you may be on a holiday or even for your PC display and never recognize you've already been offered from the industry.

In a case over, you are able to merely location an end from, state, $5. forty ($2 greater than exactly where you have within from $3. forty, but nonetheless around $2 beneath in which the share happens to be buying and selling with regard to from $7. 20) and revel in remaining in the industry. In case your choices visit $8. 20 within worth, you merely proceed your own cease as much as $6. forty.

That you can do trailing stops by hand through working upon every single day as well as modifying your own cease purchases (by carrying out a cancel/replace order). Nevertheless, there are several broker agent systems which will location the actual trailing halts for you personally. You merely let them know what lengths underneath the cost you would like your own cease, as well as it may be carried out for you personally.

Depending Purchases

This is a good purchase that's distinctive to choices. Choices on the share tend to be based on exactly where which share happens to be listed. Within the choices in the world, the share is also known as the "underlying." (In truth, you'll listen to lots of discussing "the underlying" with regards to choices ... the actual share is actually exactly what "underlies" the choices)

It means that choices alter within cost since the fundamental share modifications within cost. Choices are associated with the actual share cost. You can state choices on their personal tend to be depending on the fundamental share cost.

As well as that's exactly what the depending purchase is actually. It's merely a method to key in a good purchase to purchase a choice, but rather associated with indicating the possibility cost you would like, a person stipulate exactly where you would like the actual share in order to the industry from prior to your own purchase is activated.

Reason of learning the lingo

Now it is a question, do we need to learn the lingo?

It is a vital question for option traders. It is true that learning the lingo is essential for option traders. It is important because of the following reasons, these are given below:

Reason 1:

In order to be familiar with everything feasible concerning this perform, the professional people should also realize the actual trading policy, each like an occupation so that as a location to operate. Such as each and every occupation, you have to discover the unique language.

Reason 2:

Partially specialized, partially slang, high of its standardized about the English-speaking phase. Like an operating system professional, you have to know about this particular vocabulary, just like the auto technician has to know the titles associated with their resources.

Reason 3:

As your theater instructors, as well as company directors, may wish to talk to a person within the language from the theater when you are focusing on your own class workouts as well as within manufacturing, you're by using this on the internet appendix to go over these types of conditions.

Your own instructor may determine exactly what part of the actual lexicon from the phase you'll need instantly. The rest is going to be set aside for that period when you're really dealing with company directors within manufacturing.

Chapter 2 What Makes A Skillful Options Trader?

An option trader is any person who will buy and also markets options in the capital market. Since options trading will be performed by means of on the web alternative investing brokerages, additionally it is known as on the web options trading or perhaps on the web alternative investing. Alternative investing and also options trading and investing are very different from several ranges.

Inventory dealers acquire if the inventory increases, and also drop any time that decreases.

Nonetheless, options dealers (call and also set quality buyers) not necessarily need to find the proper course with the inventory, nevertheless the stock's shift need to take place inside a moment (before the particular expiry date). Moreover, there exists a quality integrated: the particularly meant volatility (IV): which shows us simply how much some other contact and also set dealers to assume in which inventory to go. As a result, not merely carry out these kinds of speculators will need the particular root to go inside the proper course and also in a specific timeframe.

There are many positive aspects of being able to options trading as a possible purchase method yet several positive aspects will be in which investing options needs one to devote smaller amount money to a purchase when compared to an inventory or some other form of business needs. Through the use of an alternative, you can make the maximum amount of or maybe more income much like other styles regarding investments. Now it is a question, what makes a skillful options trader?

There are lots of paths to being an expert options trader. Whenever monetary companies sponsor with regard to buying and selling jobs, these people have a tendency to consider individuals with levels within mathematics, architectural as well as difficult sciences instead of merely individuals with financial skills. There's also various buying and selling work -- a number of that need client dealing with conversation abilities around graph experienced. Nevertheless, we'll take a look at a few of the abilities which are needed of investors. Now I am going to discuss some major skills in options trading. These are given below:

Analytical Skill

If you wish to be an expert options trader, you'll have to discover and evaluate your personal buying and selling. It's hard, but you will get lots of advantages as a result. To begin with, you are able to enhance your own buying and selling as well as allow it to be much more lucrative. Next, you are able to enhance your own analytical abilities. It is important you will get through buying and selling.

If you want to investigate your own competitors, you may enhance your own analytical abilities. A good investor may evaluate and may discover disadvantages in most of the challenges. You are able to enhance your own analytical considering by utilizing unique buying and selling software program. This kind of software program will help you gather useful details about your own competitors. You'll have to evaluate these details. This will help you earn. The greater a person evaluate your own competitors the greater your own buying and selling.

Options buying and selling can provide a person great analytical considering. This will help you pull findings within hard circumstances whenever you don't have sufficient info. It's a really advantageous ability simply because the existence frequently provides us inadequate details about the problem as well as we must create a hard option. Your own analytical abilities can help you almost everywhere.

Whenever you focus on option buying and selling in the capital market, you are able to enhance your own analytical abilities. Whenever you enhance your own analytical abilities a person begins working on option buying and selling much better.

It is true that an option trader can get a chance to evaluate information rapidly. There's a large amount of mathematics involved with buying and selling, however, it is symbolized via graphs along with indications and designs through specialized evaluation. As a result, investors have to create their own analytical abilities to allow them to identify developments as well as developments within the graphs.

Research

Investors must have a proper desire with regard to info along with a need to discover all of the appropriate information which affects the investments in the capital market. Many investors produce calendars associated with financial produces as well as arranged bulletins which have measurable results about the capital marketplaces. When you are along with these types of info resources, investors can respond to brand new info since the marketplace continues to be processing this.

Indeed, on the internet trading demands just a few clicks; nevertheless, you should not really turn out to be over-zealous. Since you are somewhat taken off the procedure associated with really dealing with your hard earned money, you can easily overlook that certain incorrect click on will set you back 1000s of dollars. Rather, strategies on the internet trading while you might all of your additional expense efforts. The investigation may be crucial to ensure a person makes the most of this particular -- which will give a chance to help to make fast choices.

Focus

The focus is ability also it boosts the more investor's physical exercise this. Simply because there's a lot of monetary info available, investors require every single child develop within about the essential, actionable information which will impact their own deals. A few investors additionally focus within about the kinds of investments these people industry on allowing them to deepen their own knowledge of a particular field, business or even foreign currency to the stage exactly where this gets the aggressive benefit towards much less specific investors.

One main difficulty along with operating your choices buying and selling online businesses is actually distraction! The web is a substantial supply of info and it is common to stroll away from your own goal when you are discovering something on the internet. Trading options aren't any various, you'll probably run into an incredible number of referrals in relation to this particular subject, a few that would end up being really useful, however, the majority is only going to work like a distraction. Remain focused in your job, you are able to usually save additional web pages as well as study all of them later on. Or else you will discover that you have squandered a couple of hours on the internet, examining choices or even info you need to intuitively understand you will not make use of.

Control

Together along with concentrate is actually managed. The investor must manage his / her feelings as well as stay with the buying and selling strategy and technique. This is particularly essential within controlling danger by utilizing cease deficits or even getting earnings from arranged factors. Many methods are made therefore the investor manages to lose just a little within poor deals and methodically increases much more on great deals. Whenever investors begin to obtain psychological regarding their own deals -- great or even poor -- technique is out the actual eye-port.

Because brand new investors start in the actual marketplaces where people frequently discover there's a costly understanding contour towards the monetary marketplaces. The investor that has selected specialized evaluation since the approach to the option may quickly discover it isn't because simple because all the publications and websites allow it to seem. The actual solitary greatest cause is which buying and selling by itself are really a mental online game so when placing real cash at risk, many brand new investors stress and be the actual losers within the online game. Those people who are skilled investors recognize that is the specialized evaluation by itself function. Recognizing designs brought on by group concern or even avarice constitutes the foundation associated with specialized evaluation by itself. Brand new investors have to conquer the feelings associated with concern and avarice when they need to be being prosperous investors prior to going shattered.

Certainly, the brand new investor needs to learn how to control their own feelings. It is easier for truthful skilled investors will acknowledge it's something for these people who have a problem with nonetheless. Here are a few methods for you to learn how to keep the feelings under control:

Perfect buying and selling technique as well as stick to it. Define your own strategy in options trading. Do not begin hearing trading experts as well as their own share recommendations. Avoid the majority of share discussion boards (at minimum before you obtain self-confidence within yourself). Probably the most prosperous investors learn how to believe with regard to on their own and consider individual obligation for his or her buying and selling. Whenever you cease subsequent your own strategy and begin busting your personal guidelines you are most likely buying and selling on feeling.

Don't turn out to be psychologically mounted on your own deals. If you are viewing the buying price of your own share just like a hawk and be elated once the cost rises and stressed out once the cost falls, you are buying and selling upon feeling. Keep in mind, your own buying and selling technique ought to be therefore ingrained that you simply industry just like an automatic robot.

Take sufficient placement dimensions. Do not have a placement dimension bigger than 10 % of the accounts worth. Big placement dimensions are excellent when the cost rises however always remember that the dropping industry associated with too big the dimension may decimate your own buying and selling accounts. This can help maintain concern under control.

Remember, it is OKAY to consider the reduction. For those who have an agenda to reduce deficits, going for a reduction is simply a part of buying and selling. Actually, professionals encounter deficits. The distinction is actually they have an agenda with regard to controlling all of them.

Report Maintaining

Probably essential secrets to buying and selling are reported maintaining. If your investor information the outcomes associated with his / her deals faithfully, after that enhancing is the issue associated with screening as well as tweaking methods to locate a prosperous one. It's difficult to exhibit improvement if you're maintaining precise information.

Chapter 3   The Benefits Of Options Trading

Despite the fact that Options trading may exist some kind of dangers, it's regarded as the less dangerous method of buying and selling exactly where generating higher come back is extremely quick.

Whilst talking about on the internet buying and selling, the investor is provided the chance to begin buying and selling having a minimal amount of cash associated with $10 based on the buying and selling device selected. The Options trading is decreased since it provides the chance to the investor to get less than he is able to pay for to get rid of. In addition, the broker agent system signifies towards the investors the precise quantity that they have the chance to earn and also the quantity they'll shed, before the expense which created. When the comeback or even the possible reduction conjectures don't match the actual investor, the second option may get the chance to alter their expense to some scaled-down or even higher quantity.

Consequently, options trading provide the chance to investors to judge the actual dangers prior to these people commit their own cash, the industry function which other styles associated with the capital system doesn't supply. Regardless of just how much the capital marketplace techniques, the actual investor will be conscious of their possible deficits.

Investment for online trading

Binary options trading is more popular amongst investors on multiple websites. This particular recognition is a result of the different method of buying and selling they provide. Furthermore, the investors are able to keep track of their own on the internet buying and selling expense through buying and selling how much money they need. By doing this associated with buying and selling allows the absolute minimum expense associated with $10 for each deal, producing the internet deals on economical based on the buying and selling device selected. In addition, Options trading provides an array of capital property to purchase, for example Foreign exchange, goods, and shares.

- Foreign exchange -- That explains modifications within foreign currency, for example, UNITED STATES DOLLAR, EUR as well as AUD
- Goods -- Alloys, for example, Silver and gold, Essential oil and much more
- Shares -- They are large businesses for example Search engines as well as Apple Company that can be found in the resource checklist.

Quick Results

Nowadays investors interesting on Options trading system, wish to produce higher earnings inside a fairly brief time period. When compared with additional conventional capital buying and selling techniques, trading options creates an extremely quick come back. It provides the chance to possess a revenue border as much as 85% in the preliminary expense created. The expiration occasions on the buying and selling systems are fairly brief with respect to the buying and selling device selected. For instance, while using the Pace Option device, the expiration period generally remain in between 30 to 3 hundred mere seconds. On the other hand, conventional buying and selling are kept with regard to the lengthier time period and it can move up to many years in some instances. The chance to industry quickly on capital marketplaces combined with possible of getting higher results is the majority of appealing function associated with binary trading options. If your investor works for several successful deals, he is able to create a considerable revenue in 2 hours.

Are Options Trading Simple?

It is a million dollars question. Some people believe that it is a simple task. Now it is a question, is it simple? To be able to accelerate the procedure in the preliminary expense towards the first industry, agents possess made certain which buying and selling Options trading are easy as you possibly can. Apart from, you will find a few actions included between your putting your signature on up to and including system phase with selecting the capital resource of the investor which may decide to commit on. Individuals actions likewise incorporate the option from the quantity of the buyer really wants to industry, picking a the resource, he or she really wants to industry along with and also the path he or she believes the marketplace may proceed through the finish from the expiration period. The investor will get via each one of these phases within just a few mouse clicks on options trading software.

In addition, the revenue or even reduction the traders may experience will be based on the variances from the worth from the resource. If your investor thinks the price of the options is increasing, then he will call to his trading center. While when the investor thinks the marketplace is actually slipping, he'd commit on the "put" option. To be able to make sure that the "call" is actually lucrative, the actual shutting cost ought to be more than the actual hit cost in the expiration period. Appropriately, for any "put" to become lucrative, the cost should be the actual hit cost in the expiration period.

Are Options trading easy?

Because the majority of the buying and selling systems are web-based, they may be utilized almost everywhere with no downloading so long as the investor comes with a web connection. This particular accessibility makes it simple for that investor too frequently as well as easily examine their own options and keep track of the capital marketplace on the 24/7. Apart from, since the system provides the use of worldwide marketplaces, investors may continuously maintain buying and selling in the day time. Furthermore, the actual web-based systems are on desktop computer systems in addition to laptop computers, tabs as well as cell phones that boost the buying and selling entry. The mobile software is extremely well-liked and it is suitable for Google android as well as IOS software program.

Buying and selling Options trading may be the new pattern nowadays. This particular developing recognition, as well as notoriety, has remote instances originated from the truth that it's fairly simple to attempt this particular experience which is accessible. To prevent about the incorrect aspect from the street, the investor ought to, to begin with, help to make the comprehensive investigation to be able to pick the most dependable broker agent of the organization. Whilst talking about binary options buying and selling, the option from the company may be the toughest action for 2 factors. The first thing is simple because there's a huge quantity of trading options companies and also the 2nd cause, which is controlled and regards their own guarantee. Consequently, this particular essential option may figure out the entire trip from the investor. As soon as this task carried out, it's recommended regardless of whether you're and skilled investor or even not really to handle a few investigation concerning the capital marketplace and also to make use of the academic resources of the system that you've chosen for you.

Nowadays, more investors are coming to options trading. Many software manufacturers produce Options trading software for potential investors. This particular software program is easy to use, as well as binary trading options (broker) systems make sure this particular to ensure that customers aren't delaying.

All of you need to do forecast if the resource cost goes upward or even lower. This is something possible to discover by yourself through examining the actual capital marketplaces, as well as how you can do that is by using the program which buying and selling systems provide on the internet. Here are some advantages of utilizing binary trading options software program:

- Buying and selling software program offer marketplace info instantly, which makes it simpler that you should help to make proper conjecture generally, therefore reducing the strain or even concern with dropping your own expense.

- The program offers the establishing associated with free of charge demonstration company accounts upon which you'll exercise, once more utilizing real-time marketplace info. Therefore you may make simulated deals and obtain encounter before you decide to really start buying and selling.

- The demonstration accounts additionally allow you to check buying and selling methods. By doing this you are able to learn to make use of numerous confirmed methods and alter a few based on your look, as well as learn how to adjust all of them based on the ever-changing marketplace.

- The program additionally gives you lessons, ideas, discussion boards as well as movies with regard to assistance and assist with your own buying and selling choices. Keep in mind that the majority of agents provide free of charge demonstration company accounts, you will be anticipated to create some kind of repayment to be able to entry the program. When you register as a fellow member, it is possible to obtain the program.

- This particular software may also dual upward like a binary choice indicators supplier, allowing you to acquire information and figure out the actual asset's cost.

To become the prosperous options trading investor, you have to find out how the marketplace functions as well as realize it's developments. Using binary trading options software will help you to improve your own abilities as well as the understanding of binary trading options.

Chapter 4 Common Beginners mistakes

Options are an excellent buying and selling a device that may be found in just about all marketplace problems, possibly to create earnings, or even hedge danger. There are many brand new investors' help to make once the key in the planet associated with trading options. Whenever utilized improperly, may erode your own accounts rapidly, or even within the most detrimental situation produce border phone calls. Listed here are 7 errors newbie options investors help to make, as well as how to prevent all of them.

1. Concentrating on OTM Options

From the cash (OTM) phone or even place options are usually less expensive, a lot of investors look at all of them like a good offer. Whilst this is accurate in some instances, options are listed so that you simply aren't heading to obtain a free of charge lunch time. The high quality, or even worth from the option whenever you purchase this, decays as time passes. Consequently, the cost must not proceed over (for the phone option) or even beneath (put option) your own hit cost, however it requirements to do this prior to the option expires, as well as through sufficient in order to counteract the price of the possibility.

It may be hard to earn money with this particular strategy. Occasionally buying and selling OTM options is really a legitimate technique, however, don't obtain captured within the snare associated with convinced that simply because the possibility is less expensive and it's much better to offer compared to an additional option. Measure the likelihood how the fundamental resource may surpass the hit cost prior to expiration, depending on historic habits, prior to purchasing OTM options.

2. Define a strategy

Options are extremely versatile, as well as may be used in most marketplace problems. Although not just about all option methods work in most marketplace problems. Whenever a good fundamental resource is relaxed as well as hardly shifting, purchasing OTM phone or even place options isn't prone to create great results so long as the fundamental marketplace continues to be toned.

However, composing protected options (when you've got a placement within the fundamental share as well as create options towards it) with this atmosphere may create extra money for you personally. There's also additional methods which are more complicated, for example, Metal Condors, that include getting several jobs as well as creating a revenue in the event that the buying price of the fundamental doesn't proceed a lot. The same as share investors are trained to diversify, options investors also needs to diversify the techniques utilized. Put into action on various techniques for various marketplace problems, as well as with regard to various shares or even property depending on their own habits.

3. Lacking an exit panels

A significant mistake with regard to brand new option investors in most marketplaces really isn't getting a good exit panel. Whenever you have an industry you're looking to earn money, however how much cash? Exactly how are you going to choose the quantity of revenue that's suitable? In the event that this appears like your own option will end useless would your market to recover a few of the price, lowering your reduction? Are you going to contain the option till expiration?

Observe four Methods to Leave the Dropping Industry

They are queries which have to be tackled prior to the industry. Produce an arrangement for such a practical revenue focus on is actually, in line with the historic motion from the fundamental resource. Figure out how you'll reduce the danger, so you'll leave the industry if it's dropping as well as appears like this won't complete within the cash.

4. Unaware to promote Shifting Occasions

State a person produce a good options industry depending on peaceful marketplace situation, as well as you'll revenue so long as the fundamental resource remains docile. You'll wish to determine in the event that any kind of marketplace shifting occasions tend to be because of away within the share in the period body of the industry. A good income discharge, for instance, might toss the wrench inside your strategy, growing volatility, altering marketplace problems and placing your own "quiet times" technique needlessly at risk.

Be familiar with what's occurring within the marketplaces you're buying and selling. Main financial occasions for example given min's or even a good income discharge can alter marketplace problems rapidly, as well as your technique ought to support for your options trading. Keep track of the financial diary with income diary and produce an arrangement for the way you may industry close to main information occasions. You may choose the industry near to these types of occasions, therefore getting rid of the large unfamiliar associated with the way of the marketplace may respond to the big event.

5. Disregarding Constant Increases

Creating a large obtain on the industry is really a good sensation, however, it's also difficult to do. Within hindsight you can easily place the house operates deals, however, in real-time, it's also harder. Most of the time shares perform absolutely nothing (or absolutely nothing major), also it isn't simple to determine whenever one of these is all about to increase.

However, marketplaces continuously proceed a number of portion factors inside an issue associated with times. Consequently, producing constant scaled-down results could be simpler compared to producing one large comeback. Whilst producing 2% per week depending on a regular technique isn't because attractive like a 20% come back, you'll most likely have the ability to stand upward several 2% days prior to actually recording a large champion.

Additionally, keep in mind that each time a person create a little, as well as constant, obtain you're creating your own funds. This particular creates compounding results. However, each time a person shed on the "home run" industry you're decreasing funds, decreasing the quantity of funds readily available for deals. With time it's an extremely damaging impact since it gets tougher as well as tougher I to recover deficits because placement dimensions reduce of decreasing funds.

6. Attempting to "Time" Legged Deals

Option methods frequently need getting several options jobs simultaneously. This kind of deals needs a number of dealings, which ought to happen simultaneously to achieve the required placement. A few investors can make the actual dealings individually although, trying to improve their own revenue somewhat through obtaining one option with an uptick as well as an additional on the downtick, for instance. The issue is that you might wind up lacking your own eye-port to determine the positioning. When the cost starts to operate before you decide to establish your own jobs you might be remaining subjected to unfamiliar danger.

In the event that you're developing a placement that needs several option deals, consider all of them all at one time. Don't attempt to choose your own admittance factors. Even though this functions it'll just possess a minimal impact on general success, and may screw up the initial technique when the cost techniques towards a person when you are waiting for a much better admittance.

7. Not Addressing Created Options

Composing options is a method to generate profits, while you have the high quality through promoting the possibility in advance; when the option expires useless you're able to keep your whole quantity obtained. The high quality may be the optimum revenue although, and when the fundamental resource will go towards a person, a person possibly encounter big deficits (this is the reason why the majority of option authors possess a placement within the fundamental resource too, known as protected option writing). The error from the option author is faltering to secure a few of the high quality once they possess the opportunity.

In the event, you marketed alternatives with $2. 00 and will escape the particular business if the quality will be $0. 45 meaning an individual nonetheless arrive at retain 80% with the authentic quality an individual acquired (fewer commissions): an individual nonetheless pants pocket $1. 58 multiplied simply by how many explains to you regarding explains to you an individual published alternatives about. Preserving 80% surpasses probably being forced to pay above funds (or the inventory in the event the alternative will be covered) in the event the value should go in opposition to an individual just before expiry.

The underside Collection

Options really are an excellent device, functional in the most marketplace problems; however, they may be devastating if your investor doesn't learn how to put into action on these types of monetary devices correctly. Diversify your own methods as well as get ready for possible modifications within marketplace problems which may be powered through main information occasions. Understand how you'll leave deals, as well as concentrate on constant results more than house operates deals. In case your placement demands several option deals, perform all of them simultaneously; faltering to do this might endanger the actual technique. Whenever you create options, don't hesitate to leave the actual industry as well as maintain the main high quality, particularly when there is the query regarding if the option may end useless or even not really.

Chapter 5 The Principles of Pricing

Traders may use options to obtain earnings through non-dividend-paying shares to buy a share as well as restrict for its danger. Investors may use options to include influence by having a suitable degree of danger that's genuinely restricted, in addition to industry upward, lower as well as range-bound marketplaces.

In spite of these types of advantages as well as constantly developing quantity (more compared to 15% substance quantity development because 1973), options continue to be within their childhood concerning open public knowing as well as popularity.

Listed here are 10 crucial concepts which beginners to options ought to bear in mind because they make plan for the options industry. Now I am going to discuss these concepts.

Concept 1

Understand the distinction in between utilizing options to get as well as utilizing options to industry: Traders concentrate on the advantages of long-term share possession, and they ought to make use of options to purchase, market, or even safeguard share jobs, in order to improve earnings through share jobs. Think about a good buyer likely to purchase share whenever he or she gets the year-end reward. This particular buyer can purchase 1 phone these days for every 100 gives he or she programs to buy. The phone option is really an agreement that provides the customer to purchase the fundamental share in the hit cost any time before termination day. Basically, it is with regard to having to pay the price of the shares for these days. When the share cost is greater once the buyer gets the actual reward, he then nevertheless can buy the planned-for quantity of gives. With no phone, the amount of gives would need to end up being decreased provided the larger share cost.

Investors, as opposed to traders, tend to be short-term marketplace timers along with small curiosity about having the fundamental share, and they frequently make use of a higher level of influence. Bought options provide investors the possibility of substantial influence along with restricted danger. However, the danger is real. Options may shed 50% or even more of the cost very quickly in the event that the buying prices of the fundamental share techniques the wrong manner. Additionally, out-of-the-money options end useless from termination for any complete lack of the cost compensated, in addition, profits.

Concept 2

Traders, that make use of options require a strategy: May the bought option end up being worked out or even offered if it's in-the-money from termination? Protected authors have to know whether they are prepared to market the fundamental share. Otherwise, it is advisable to choose ahead of time from exactly what cost the phone call is going to be repurchased or even folded to an additional option.

Concept 3

Know how as well as the reason why option costs later: Option costs later in a different way compared to share costs, therefore option investors have to strategy in a different way compared to share investors. An average problem through beginners to options is real: "The share proceeded to go upward, however, my personal phone didn't! Focusing on how costs alter is important to utilizing options effectively.

The worth associated with time provides theoretical ideals of the 50-strike phone from various share costs and various times to termination provided the mentioned presumptions regarding rates of interest, returns as well as volatility. Each one of the series within the desk is really a various share cost, as well as each one of the posts is really a various quantity of times to termination. This discloses 2 essential ideas regarding option costs -- the idea of "delta" which associated with "non-linear period rot.

The idea of "delta" is which for any $1 alter within the fundamental share cost, the worthiness of the phone can change through under $1. Within "The worth of your time, when the share cost increases through $50 to $51 from 3 months, the $50 increases through 50¢. Delta explains the anticipated alter within an option's cost for any $1 alter within the fundamental stock's cost, which means this is referred to as using a delta associated with 0. 50.

The desk demonstrates which option costs don't reduce at the exact same price after a while to termination, presuming elements besides time for you to termination stay continuous. Think about the middle strip where the share is $50. Because the time for you to termination reduces through 50% through 3 months to forty-five times, the worthiness from the $50 phone reduces through around 31% through $3. 20 in order to $2. Twenty-five. It's this that "non-linear period erosion" indicates.

Searching throughout any kind of strip, you will see how the reduction in the passing of your time, so-called period erosion or even theta, differs based on regardless of whether an option is in-the-money, at-the-money or even out-of-the-money.

Concept 4

Option investors require self-discipline within getting earnings as well as deficits: Very first, possess a revenue focus on as well as near or even decrease how big a situation in the event that which cost is actually arrived at. 2nd, possess a stop-loss stage as well as near or even decrease how big a situation from which cost. 3rd, possess a time period limit as well as near or even decrease how big a situation in the event that nor the actual revenue focus on neither the stop-loss stage tends to be arrived at through the finish of times time period.

Concept 5

Don't get freaked away through volatility: Conceptually, options act like insurance coverage, and also the volatility element in options refers towards the danger element in insurance coverage. It's a key point, however, it's not the only real element. Whilst the idea of volatility isn't without effort apparent in order to beginners, it may be discovered in the event that the first is individual.

Concept 6

It possesses practical anticipation: Learning the actual ideas associated with delta as well as theta (time decay) is definitely an essential action towards the aim of building practical anticipation about how exactly option costs may as well as may not alter as well as just how much revenue possible as well as danger every technique offers.

Concept 7

Buying undervalued options as well as selling over-valued options aren't adequate methods: "Value" is really a very subjective dedication that each investor should help to make separately. Option investors should concentrate on their own three-part predict around or even more compared to "value" of the option.

Concept 8

Selling options" isn't a much better technique compared to "buying options": It's a fantasy which 80-90% associated with options end useless. Around 1 / 3, or even 33%, associated with options end useless whilst 10-15% tend to be worked out. The remainder will be shut just before termination. Whilst option composing (selling) could be a prosperous technique, beginners frequently misunderstand this. There's a cause, there's a high quality to take upon much more danger. There isn't any solution to it -- option purchasers spend reasonably limited associated with described danger as well as option retailers get a high quality to take on danger.

Concept 9

Influence is really a double-edged blade: Option investors ought to handle their own funds in a different way compared to share investors. Your decision is to buy two hundred gives off the trading from $50 for each reveal is extremely various how the option to buy 100 phone trading options from $1 every, despite the fact that each deal includes a good expense associated with $10, 000, excluding profits. Usually, options investors may commit an inferior part of complete funds to every industry. Option investors, nevertheless, may have much more open up jobs compared to share investors.

Concept 10

Create a marketplace predicting method through beginning little, recognizing earnings with deficits as well as through operating at a constant speed: Investors will be able to clarify their own trade-selection procedure inside a couple of phrases. New people can deal which have just little possible earnings as well as deficits, simply because this can improve their own likelihood of sustaining objectivity. Deals should be started and shut to ensure that the trading rhythm is created.

Almost any person may learn how to work on options trading when they invest a couple of hours in each week on their own method. However, you may invest many years without having learning options. Discover these types of concepts as well as go one action at any given time. Options tend to be such as levels of the red onion -- there's always something a new comer to discover. Don't grow to become discouraged as well as, more to the point, don't turn out to be more than assured and believe you realize everything simply because you will get burnt.

Chapter 6 Options Trading Strategies For Beginners

Share investment, options trading, as well as foreign currency buying and selling -- they are a few of the well-liked methods for producing extra earnings apart from selecting the standard methods. Now it is a question, what types of methods we will choose.

Therefore you are currently acquainted with share investment as well as options trading. You do not think of attempting all of them however you'd be happy to understand some possible causes of investment earnings. And thus, your own desire is my personal order! A person arrived right here simply because you need to understand a few information about Options trading. This short article will not make you a specialist about them, however, it can easily provide you a solution of the easiest queries you have now. You don't need to defeat your own minds away!

Foreign currencies are essential to many people in some other part of the world. They're required to operate international companies. For instance, you're a visitor from the United States and want to vacation in European countries. Obviously, you can't spend a large amount of money to visit the most popular holiday destinations presently there. You will have to trade your dollars for that nearby foreign currency.

This is why there's constant have to trade foreign currencies. For this reason truth, Currency markets are just about the greatest capital marketplace in the world.

A few Benefits of Options trading

Therefore, you are able to obtain earnings. Exactly what is to otherwise? Why is this kind of buying and selling much better for a person?

You can test a totally free demonstration accounts

This really is good for the new person as if you're a little uncertain regarding yourself. Attempting a totally free demonstration accounts prepares a person for that period which you will have to commit your hard earned money within the expectations of getting actual earnings. It can help you determine in the event that options trading is perfect for a person.

The marketplace deals twenty-four hours in a day

Therefore, you do not intend to get it done full-time. That is simply good. You are able to do it anytime from the day time since the marketplace in no way sleeps.

There is not any fixed dimension

Wish to take part having a great deal dimension, let's imagine, $25? Not a problem! A person figures out your personal placement dimension.

Presently there you have this; the actual group of fundamental bits of details about options trading. Would you like to check it out? Or even would you like to find out more comprehensive details? A person should pick the second option for the time being. There are many points you should know, and you ought to take advantage of your assets. Certainly, you have to be careful within attempting to invest. It will pay to become daring sufficient to consider dangers. Simply be sure you include sufficient understanding of exactly what you are performing.

You need to attempt your own hands from binary trading options. Within options trading, you won't work as the participant, however, a good buyer spends the cash inside a strong task to generate. That's the reason binary trading options methods are your primary tool. There's a large group of this kind of methods, if you wish to be successful, you have to positively discover as well as utilize those that you prefer and appear guaranteeing. Try to follow the instruction along with easy options trading techniques for newcomers. It ought to be remembered which options trading is the main huge as well as the complex system --

the actual capital marketplace, that is not really disorderly as well as arbitrary, however, the Options trading market works based on particular regulations. Now I am going to discuss some strategies for Options trading for newcomers, these techniques are given below:

Diversity Technique

Caused by the possibility is determined by the overall scenario on the market and also the particular present cost for any specific resource. Just by making use of particular binary trading options technique, an investor may industry effectively and thus, generate upon their opportunities.

Keep in mind that any kind of technique, actually apparently win-win, can't work preferably constantly. Losing can be done and you will generate losses, however, more to the point, don't shed all at one time. Permitting the chance associated with episodic subsidence associated with funds, you shouldn't place all of the cash into 1 option. It's very dangerous as well as careless. Preferably, you ought to have the money, a minimum of 10 investments. This type of sensible as well as the wise mindset is in the direction of down payment known as money diversity. Allow the thought of diversity never simply leaves the mind.

5 Minutes Technique

This tactic is simple, might state actually a good primary easy, which is well suited for newbies who've absolutely no encounter, absolutely no severe funds upon down payment. It doesn't assure 100 % associated with achievement, however, it's likelihood, based on traditional estimations, is near to 80 %. Throughout the day, you should use this frequently, growing, therefore, your own little funds unless of course, obviously, you're very sensible, as well as best of luck won't change from a person.

5 Min's technique is dependent on the truth that many agents permit you to purchase options on the severe degree -- within 5 min's prior to the termination. All that's necessary would be to rummage around the property on the market in order to find one which is actually steady and

developing for a long period or even, on the other hand, reduces. Remember to find it's optimum worth, that, without a doubt, this time around can be a switching stage for that pattern, as well as arrived at the historical higher, the pattern most likely can change the movement towards the reverse.

Martingale

The actual theory from the Martingale is actually regarded as much less dangerous and secure whenever buying and selling options trading. Martingale theory is dependent on doubling the next quantities when the prior industry is unsuccessful. That's, should you shed $100, you need to industry once again along with some $200. Should you shed $200, it's the period simply to place $400. You need to your own buying and selling quantity if you earn, or else all of the prior deals to show the really substantial reduction.

Martingale and Kelly Theory

Consequently, to use the actual theory associated with Martingale within its finest type, depending on good fortune, is extremely dangerous. You need to discover the foreign currency set, having a cleanup or even lower pattern associated with cost motion. It's reasonable to presume this pattern won't alter soon. You need to use this particular short-term balance. It's much more dependable to options trading through Martingale theory utilizing binary option indications. Options trading indicators currently provide you with an opportunity to earn, as well as while using theory associated with Martingale you'll significantly improve this.

Quarter-hour Technique

You need to monitor a good resource on quarter-hour time-frame, in the event that all of us observe 3 or even more consecutive candle lights from the exact same color, let's await the rollback. We ought to purchase binary option following two min's dreaming about moving back again. For instance, all of us observe 3 whitened candle lights shut, brand new candlestick starts also it gets into the alternative path -- the cost reduces. All of us wait around 2 min's to create and repair it folded back again.

Triangle

Triangles will vary, however they display the impending discovery cost. The number of items is increasing, portend the impending improve within costs along with a split up, however slipping triangles, on the other hand, tend to be harbingers associated with its most likely drop. Appropriately, investors need to improve or even loss of the cost whenever you observe the actual graph offers created the actual related determine. To determine this, industry ought to aesthetically pull 2 outlines with the factors associated with the opposition as well as assistance. Opposition collection (higher) should be horizontally and assistance collection is situated from a good position. It's apparent which inside a downtrend, investors possess to consider the downwards triangle. Within climbing down triangle, assistance collection is horizontal, opposition collection got rid of from a good severe position into it -- on optimum factors.

Conclusion

Nowadays, many investors' portfolios consist of opportunities, for example, shared money, shares as well as provides. However, all of the investments you've available don't finish presently there. Another kind of protection, known as an option, provides a global associated with the chance to advanced traders.

The ability associated with options is based on their own flexibility. These people allow you to adjust or even change your situation based on any kind of scenario which occurs. Options are often as risky or even because traditional while you would like. What this means is that you can do from safeguarding a situation from the decrease to downright wagering about the motion of the marketplace or even catalog.

This particular flexibility, nevertheless, doesn't arrive without having its expenses. Options are complicated investments as well as can be dangerous.

Options include dangers and therefore are not really ideal for everybody. Options buying and selling could be risky within character as well as have considerable danger associated with reduction. Just commit along with danger funds.

In spite of exactly what anyone lets you know, option buying and selling entail danger, particularly if you do not understand what you do. Due to this, lots of people recommend a person avoid options as well as overlook their own living.

However, becoming uninformed associated with any kind of expense locations inside a fragile placement. Probably the risky character associated with options does not match your look. Not a problem -- after that do not theorize within options. However, before you decide to choose not really to purchase options, you need to realize all of them. Not really understanding exactly how options perform is really as harmful because leaping correct within: without having the understanding regarding options you'd not just lose getting an additional product inside your trading toolkit but additionally shed understanding to the operation associated with a few of the planet's biggest companies. Now it is your decision to think about it.

Did you know that a large percent of people who make a lot of money lose it within the first couple years?

It doesn't take much for a person to lose all of their money. Around 2 in 3 lottery winners lose all of their winnings within 5 years. If someone could lose hundreds of millions of dollars over a couple years, how fast will you lose your millions that you could make from this book?

Over the past couple years I have stumbled upon the key secret behind managing money and KEEPING it. If you follow the link below you will uncover the truth behind managing and keeping the money you make

>>> Click/Tap here to Learn the Secret Behind Money Management
<<<

The Predictable Stock Trading System

Turn 1 Hour Of Stock Trading Per Day Into Generational Wealth

By Stephen Smith

are done without written consent and can in no way be considered an endorsement from the trademark holder.

Introduction

Congratulations on downloading *Stock Trading* and thank you for doing so.

The following chapters will discuss what the stock market is and how you can get the most out of it by trading and trading. When it comes to making an investment, there are a lot of things to consider, and this book wants to get into details about every aspect needed to take conscious and smart decisions.

For all those who are looking for a complete guide on how to trade today, I wanted to create this book to find all the information useful for their investment and to avoid a possible scam! Below, I will analyze the possibility of trading today safely.

There are plenty of books on this subject on the market, thanks again for choosing this one! Every effort was made to ensure it is full of as much useful information as possible, please enjoy!

Did you know that a large percent of people who make a lot of money lose it within the first couple years?

It doesn't take much for a person to lose all of their money. Around 2 in 3 lottery winners lose all of their winnings within 5 years. If someone could lose hundreds of millions of dollars over a couple years, how fast will you lose your millions that you could make from this book?

Over the past couple years I have stumbled upon the key secret behind managing money and KEEPING it. If you follow the link below you will uncover the truth behind managing and keeping the money you make

>>> Click/Tap here to Learn the Secret Behind Money Management <<<

Or Go to https://secretstomoneymanagement.gr8.com/

Chapter 1
Basics for Beginners

This book will be a reference point for all traders, especially for all those who want to trade today but do not know where to start. This is, therefore, a guide mainly for beginners but not only where only the main topics will be addressed. In particular, it will take care from the beginning, to develop a complete guide dedicated to the basics of trading and to learn how and where to trade today.

Today, we live in the age of information technology and digitization, and this can only encourage investment. For this reason, today more than ever, that knowledge is all that is needed to trade simply and safely.

For all those who are looking for a quick and detailed way to trade today, we must not ignore it. Today, thanks to the evolution of new technologies, it is possible to trade directly from home, with online trading or directly on the stock exchange. Thanks to the Internet, new forms of investment were born, increasingly accessible and fast. Today, it is also possible to trade thanks to social trading.

Caution

Trading from home quickly and easily today does not presuppose the fact that it is easy. One should not fall into the temptation to believe that obtaining success in the practice of trading is easy and above all is exempt from risks.

Despite the evolution, the possibility of more information and more training on how and where to trade today does not presuppose the guaranteed success, but the possibility of success or failure has always remained more or less the same. It all depends on you, your training, and your dedication to trading.

How to Trade Today?

Between yesterday and today, what has changed is the way to trade money, which is the possibility for a beginner to access the necessary resources much more easily and better understand what to trade in today.

Here is the reason for this book, supported by practical examples and regulated and authorized brokers. You will find a series of useful information to better understand how and where to trade today, a step-by-step guide that will explain how and why trade in one industry today rather than another.

Starting to trade today is easy, simple, and fast! Doing it in the right way instead is a bit more difficult, especially if you do not have the right knowledge.

Where to Trade Today?

How many of you have asked yourselves this question and how many of you right now are asking? Understanding where to trade today is the technique for success! In fact, knowing where and how to trade implies a saving of time and a greater income for you traders, who will leave already in advance of the other traders, and this will lead you to become an advanced and successful trader.

In this guide, we will show you which market is the most accessible to all, the Forex, which will allow you to trade even with little savings. We will also show you what is Social Trading, which is a new form of investment based on Forex, and the sharing of information and trading strategies that will allow you to trade and become an expert in this market.

Chapter 2
Let's Talk About Capital

How Much to Trade Today?

Another fundamental point before starting to trade is understanding how much you are willing to trade today. The amount of capital that you are willing to trade changes according to the trader's economic resources but also to the degree of preparation.

For this reason, we consider it useful to advise you to start trading with a demo account, or a free trading account, which allows you to understand what are the risks of online trading but, above all, to feel the trading strategies or even just doing knowledge with the trading platform.

Given this, let's examine how much to trade today.

Trading capital today requires the following:

- The possibility of making use of its capital
- Use financial resources in fruit-bearing operations

How Much is the Capital Needed to Start Trading Today?

Many traders associate the meaning of a large sum of money to the term "capital." Obviously, there is not an equal capital for everyone, but every trader decides to trade his capital, according to what are the possibilities. So, for a basic level trader, trading €100 is equivalent to an experienced trader trading €1000.

Capital, therefore, is a relative amount for each of us. Almost always, however, capital, in its most general meaning, takes the form of a value that is very difficult to obtain and use for a possible investment. Today, we can tell you exactly what the world of online trading has become accessible to everyone, even to traders who do not have immense amounts of capital.

How Much to Trade for Tangible Results?

There are brokers that offer the possibility of trading in the stock market even with only €100 of initial capital, which is a ridiculous amount, that allows you not only to experience the world of online investment but also to get rid of wrong beliefs that online trading or stock exchange investment is only for those who own money. This is called a "test capital."

To understand this concept, we consider it to be of fundamental importance; if one understands it, the very concept of capital takes on a different meaning; in fact, it will mean every meaning of greatness or importance. In other words, the concept of capital will mean only the amount of money that is available and in the case of wrong investment does not affect the economic situation of the trader.

Be careful not to confuse this concept with the wrong concept of trading money in the wrong way. In reverse, you will have to treat the money you will trade with the utmost respect, giving it the utmost importance. Just constantly remind yourself that you earned that money by working hard; you do not want to waste it.

Remember that trading in online trading is risky and undermines the loss of the entire capital. So, pay close attention to this concept. It does not matter what the amount to trade or what capital is available. The important is to understand the value of the capital you trade.

If you follow this advice, you can find out how easy and quick to do online trading or trade in the stock market in a few steps and, especially like all of this today, how it is really affordable for everyone, thanks to the Internet. There is nothing left but to continue this path and make yours the information in this guide on how to trade today. When it comes to investment strategies, the amount invested cannot be ignored.

This chapter is oriented to the management of assets between 10,000 and one million Euros. Another premise for reading is to have a clear idea of what is meant by the amount investable.

We will divide our field of action into three bands. All three bands will assume that it has already been done:

1. Invest the maximum tax-deductible share in the supplementary pension
2. Stipulate any life insurance, which indicates that all the negative points described in the Life Insurance should be considered
3. Deduct from the investable portion any allowances for false investments, i.e., secondary activities that are genuine alternative works

The last point is particularly important for investments in real estate and land. As we will see in the operational plans, for assets up to €250,000, a speech on property and land can only be marginal.

The main reasons for the previous statement are the following:

1. Such investments often tend not to be real.

In the modern sense, an investment is such if it requires a minimum allocation of resources (for example, I buy 10,000 Euros of government bonds); otherwise, it is configured as a real activity.

Buying a home that you can then rent is the simplest example. If we interact directly with the tenant, we are doing a real activity, an alternative to our work, in which we often do not take into account the management costs and the time we spend; different is the case in which we limit ourselves to buying the house and entrust to a paid external structure the role of administrator of the building. In this second case, what remains is the real gain of the rent. The same applies when buying agricultural land; only by considering it an activity (i.e., cultivating it and managing it with appropriate decisions) will we make the most of it.

2. These investments minimize management costs only for large capital.

In fact, the realized capital gains are gross of the taxes and of all the management expenses that serve to maintain the asset in question over the years. For small investments (for example, a house worth 300,000 Euros)—inflation, taxes, maintenance costs, etc.—they reduce the real gain considerably.

Investment Instruments

As investment tools, consider the following:

1. Properties and land
2. Instruments for maximum liquidity (i.e., liquidable in up to three months)
3. Bonds
4. Stocks

The individual instruments must then be optimized following the instructions given in the following paragraphs.

We must warn against investing in alternative and typically speculative fields (art, jewelry, etc.) without having a specific capacity. These fields are, in fact, similar to alternative work: buying a painting, a prestigious watch, or a classic car; hoping for a great revaluation is completely optimistic if you are not an expert in the sector. On the other hand, if one is, it makes no sense to make it all occasional, but it would make sense to make it at least a second activity.

The proposed management is mainly passive; in the sense that we must follow the trend of our investments not continuously over time but with periodic checks (for example, quarterly) to verify whether it is appropriate to positively disinvest. For example, if a bond was bought a year ago at 95.25 and is now worth 99, a 4% gain justifies the sale; if, on the contrary, it has fallen to 94.20, it will put the heart in peace and will be held until its expiration.

From 10,000 to 50,000 Euros

We all know that it is disappointing by those who thought of diversifying, but with such a modest sum, you can only use two tools: those for maximum liquidity and bonds. You can use together or, better, use the latter unless the former is no longer advantageous due to a particular economic situation.

From 50,000 to 250,000 Euros

Here, the four instruments are all usable, obviously with due consideration.

For buildings and land, it is advisable to include them in the additional quota. If you decide to invest 50,000 Euros in real estate, instead of buying a tiny studio, it makes more sense to buy a bigger house of ownership; the fees on the added quota are less than on a second home, and there would not be all the hassles of managing an asset that, due to its small size, would yield modest yields in any case of a certain management commitment.

Also, in this case, the bonds take the largest share of the investable amount (at least 50%) and can be replaced by the instruments for maximum liquidity only in exceptional cases in which they make more.

The actions deserve separate speech. In theory, with a capital of €250,000, it would be possible to invest in the shareholder, but in practice, it is better to do so by linking the figure to one's age.

If at 30 years, an invested share of 40% can be significant; at the age of 60, it should not exceed 10%; with these data, it is automatic to remember that at the age of 40, a maximum of 30% is invested, and at most 20%, a maximum of 20%. We propose you the rule of 70: the sum between age and shareholding always makes 70.

Let us remember, however, that investing in the stock is an opportunity, not an obligation.

From 250,000 to One Million Euros

We are now in important figures. Before going into detail, it is necessary to understand "what wind it pulls." Currently, with an economy still in partial crisis, it seems that the situation is this:

secure bonds and liquidity: ****

actions: **

gold: **

properties: *

This picture will appear disappointing to those who dream of speculating with their capital, but it is certainly the one that protects it most.

With regard to property and land, up to 30% of assets can be invested in them, both as an additional share and as an investment in its own right. Many would come to invest up to 100%, but it is a too simplistic solution because, in fact, with such capital, if you want to invest in the brick, it makes more sense to undertake a real second activity. Furthermore, it should be remembered that *a property has value only if you can resell it!*

What in recent years has not been so easy and has produced losses of even 50%, just to fall from the investment made with a little liquidity.

In other words, instead of investing in a couple of luxury apartments in the city center, it is more logical to invest in smaller units by diversifying the risks that are always present on the individual investment. In any case, the crisis in the real estate sector that began in 2008 has, in fact, extinguished optimism that lasted for decades, optimism without a real rational motivation.

Once the portion allocated to property and land has been determined, the amount to be invested in shares must be determined; also, in this case, the maximum is represented by the rule of 70. The remaining part is destined to the bonds.

Let's See Some "Sensible" Cases.

James, 37,—investable amount €350,000—decides to have an additional share of 100,000 Euros to his house and invests 20% in shares (70,000 Euros) and the remainder in bonds (180,000).

Sara, 45,—investor 450,000—decides not to have an additional quota, buys a 110,000 euro housing unit that rents, invests 10% in shares (45,000 Euros), 260,000 Euros in bonds, and 35,000 Euros in an online account now particularly cheap.

Patrick, 42,—investable amount 700,000—decides to have a house a little bigger for his family (additional share of 100,000 Euros) and invests a 25% in shares (175,000) and the rest all in bonds, well 425,000 Euros.

Donald, 60,—investable amount €1,000,000—The house does not change it; not particularly trusting in real estate investing, it invests 100,000 Euros in shares, 100,000 in an online account, 50,000 in a normal bank account, and a good 750,000 Euros in bonds, suitably diversified.

Chapter 3
How to Use Money

Understanding that investment must earn money for those who trade them is a fundamental concept. Although it may seem rather trivial, not no is and above all not all are of the same idea. Understanding which sectors to bet on is not trivial!

There are two possible ways to trade money. Trading money also means making money work for you. Here is, therefore, explained the reason for why trading money.

In fact, we know that money is one of the major components of the budget of every single man. Money serves and is the basis of a myriad of fundamental activities that belong to our lives.

The two roads to follow are divided between:

1. Have the money
2. Use the money

To better explain these concepts, let's make a trivial example.

It is commonplace to say: Put the savings under the mattress. This concept, although quite trivial, makes us understand how this method makes us owners of money.

However, owning money does not require any investment. For them to yield, they must be traded. The money must, therefore, be used, or traded, not just hold. This is especially true when considering the constant loss of value cash undergoes every year due to inflation. Trading can be seen as a way to betting against money itself, and this is what I tend to think about when considering an opportunity.

How to Use the Capital to Trade?

It is possible to use the money to go shopping, to buy consumer goods, such as a new smartphone, a new car, or even other consumer goods. Even having a small amount of money deposited in the bank or other investment funds, however, is not a wrong solution. In all these cases, money is traded and yields. Here is the concept that explains how to use the money to make more money. This is precisely the concept of trading today.

If you use the money to trade in investment funds, it is sure that they are used to make money. In this case, producing money does not require much effort and no new initiative on your part. We only have to hope that the markets we have invested in are always positive, that is, they always close with a gain for us. Of course, it does not mean that you can forget and forget about it, but you will always be the ones to decide how and where to trade them.

To do this, you rely on financial magnates or choose to trade in online trading or other markets, thanks to online brokers, who offer you a complete training on the markets and online trading, which will then allow you to trade your money and make your capital the right choices based on those that are your strategies.

Thanks to the training courses, you will be aware of some theoretical and technical factors. The more information you have, the greater the chances of earning for you.

Trading Money Today: Two Ways to Trade Money

We can divide the investment into the two big categories:

1. Buy a good, wait for its value to increase, and then resell it at a higher value so that you can even make a profit. In this case, most traders buy and sell real estate.
2. Trading by buying shares. In this case, the trader becomes the owner of a piece of the company for which he has taken out an action, with the hope that the value of the stock will rise so that he can then sell his stock to a new buyer or shareholder and collect the profit.

At the moment, the focus will be more on this last aspect, as we consider the most developed and certainly will be the one that allows greater diversification of the portfolio.

Trading in the stock market today is also possible, thanks to options trading. In this case, thanks to the options trading, it is possible to trade in shares and also earn downwards. Buying a financial instrument of this type, therefore, allows you to earn even if the value of this goes down.

Another widely used strategy to trade today and to capitalize on its capital is to lend money for a certain period of time and then receive it with interest. Today, we talk a lot about this sector and especially about bond investment.

Investing in Bonds

When we talk about bond investment, we are certainly talking about investment in Italian bots, or English bonds, or German bunds.

Purchasing an American bot means lending to the state your money for the value of the bot at that time. The state will subsequently undertake to return them on a specific date, with the addition of pre-established interests, without the possibility of escaping this payment.

Another example is the purchase of bonds. In this way, you lend your money to the company that issued the bonds. It is not just a matter of state bodies, but also of private bodies. In this sense, the company will compensate us after a certain period by paying us an interest in the form of coupons.

These are currently the easiest ways to trade today, of alternative methods to commit your money, and make money with them. In the following chapter, we will also continue to talk about sectors in which to trade today, each category, with its own merits and defects.

Chapter 4
What Trading is NOT

Once you understand what it means to trade today, your money, it is of fundamental importance, even understand what is not an investment! Above all, understand how you must trade your money but also understand what an investment IS NOT. This last concept is not familiar to everyone; in fact, in most cases, they do not even recognize it.

Please note that trading in online trading is not the same as gambling. It is a form of pure investment, which involves its risks but which must not be compared to gambling.

You do not choose to trade in a company as I would choose a number at the casino roulette. To trade, you need to know the trend of the market and what it entails.

Unfortunately, many traders still make this mess. So, here is the wrong term to play on the stock exchange rather than trade in the stock market. This difference is not unimportant.

The art of trading is essentially based on reasonable expectations, which derive mainly from statistics or from professional studies done in that sector.

An investment is based on essential components:
1. Study
2. Experience
3. Certain facts

Obviously, the risk when trading always exists but cannot be compared to gambling. There are statistics as there are systems that work thanks to the fact that they are able to produce a profit in the best possible way and in the shortest possible time.

Therefore, the trader will have to learn to know and to favor those investment systems that statistically, in the long run, are winners. Never forget the risk associated with online trading. Only by accepting and living with the risk can we trade seriously and in a balanced way. It is, therefore, knowing the risk that it can be controlled and managed.

Tools for Financial Investment

Given the above, we will go into more specific, to learn more about what are safe investment today. Many also ask what are the main methods of common investment for a person of medium and low level, with a modest budget if not limited, and especially if it exists, something simple to start with, perhaps in a very short time?

With all frankness, that there is nothing difficult but only a complex that does not mean you cannot do it! The world of finance is constantly evolving; the classical methods of investment, even if they have not waned, have been greatly reduced and have given way to these new forms of investment.

Knowing most of it is one of the first rules for a good investment. The first rule to diversify risk is by diversifying the portfolio or trading in different types of assets.

Trading Shares as an Investment Tool

A title representing a share of a company's property is called stock. Owning one or more shares of a public limited company also implies the possibility of earning with it, as a member of that company. In this case, we speak of being a shareholder and expressing one's right to vote, having the right to earn from the profits produced by that company, to an extent that is proportional to the number of shares held.

Trading Shares

For example, if you own 1% in a company's shares, you can collect 1% when the company decides to distribute the so-called dividends.

Pay attention, however, to the fact that not all companies are equal, and there is also a diversification regarding the payment of dividends to its shareholders. In that case, those holding their own shares will be able to capitalize on their investment by earning the increase in value of their shares or even by the subsequent sale of these shares to another trader.

The stocks of this company must, however, be subject to fundamental laws of the market, related to supply and demand, but above all, we must remember that the more a society is strong, the stronger its action will be; as a result, their value will tend to grow. In the opposite case, on the other hand, in the case in which the weakness of the company will be greater, the less will be the attraction for those actions.

In short, this means that if an action does not pay dividends, it is possible that gains are obtained with the increase in value of these, by retrading or speculating on the differential between the selling price and the purchase price. The percentages of return in this case on the investment are very high, but there is also the fact that there are many risks, as well as the possibility that this does not go up in value, or worse, that it loses.

Trading Bonds

If, instead, you decide to trade in bonds, as we mentioned earlier, it means trading in debt securities. These securities are issued by companies or public bodies, which allow the holder to have the right to obtain a repayment of the principal lent to the issuer at maturity, plus an interest in this sum.

Possession of Italian bonds or btp, or English bonds, means, having lent money to a company or even to a state and then have in hand, a title that certifies the debt owed to you and that will then have to pay by a specific date. This, therefore, also presupposes a payment of a preestablished interest to honor the aforementioned loan.

In most cases, the greater the risk of the insolvency company, the greater the interest will be. In the opposite case, the lower the risk, the lower the interest will be.

But there is also another case where interests may be greater. In this case, not necessarily the company must be insolvent, but it may also happen that this is less tempting than others, and in this case, the customer will put into circulation bonds that pay a greater interest.

The most famous bonds I mention are the following:

- Italian government bonds, BOTs or BTPs
- German bonds
- American or English bonds

Trading Common Funds

Those who instead opt for trading in sound investment mutual funds that can use financial instruments that are also defined as shares of investment funds and that collect the money of savers who entrust the management of their savings to the companies of management, which have legal personality and capital different from those of the fund.

In short, when you trade in a fund, you choose to become part of a group of people, who have collected their money together. These, in turn, deliver their money to an experienced trader to get it managed.

The manager's arduous task will be to understand, with which capital he has been given, which shares and bonds to buy; in this way, the mutual fund will be built. Based on your stake in that fund, earnings will be distributed.

At the moment, there are different types of funds. In this sense, we can distinguish the following:

1. Funds that trade on baskets of securities
2. Funds that tend to replicate indices or a set of indices
3. Passively managed funds
4. Actively managed funds as well as hedge funds.

In most cases, the funds are linked to provisioning plans or insurance policies that are subscribed by users, who are not willing to spend their time to understand how and where to trade.

Advantages and Disadvantages of Mutual Funds

At the moment, there are many advantages linked to mutual funds but also many disadvantages. Among the main disadvantages, there is the fact that the returns related to the investment are often mediocre, penalized in many cases also by the high running costs. The manager must be paid, even if no profits are obtained. For this reason, management risks are always lurking. As Anthony Robbins once stated, 96% of mutual funds do not beat or draw the market in 10 years.

On the opposite side, however, there are several advantages, especially for those who have a large investment capacity. In this case, those who use the mutual funds, use them to keep the capital protected from inflation and also why not, to earn something. In much more elementary terms, inflation means higher prices for goods and services. This means a reduction of purchasing power.

In short, if today with the assets set aside you can buy a certain number of goods and services, does not mean that in a few years with the same money, you can buy them anyway. This for the simple reason that the price of those goods and services will be increased due to inflation. In technical terms, this also means a decrease in purchasing power.

Speculative Investment Instruments

Until now, I have seen three categories of investment that include the actual purchase of an asset, regardless of whether it is an action, a security, or a share, which must be held and held pending generate returns due precisely to appreciation.

Below, however, is a list of a series of tools that do not provide for the purchase of an asset, but above all, it is not necessarily due to things that the asset should be appreciated to generate a profit. In this case, we are talking about speculative investment and short selling. These presuppose the possibility of earning also following the depreciation of a particular asset.

In most cases, traders and investors talk about these investments, as well as investment in derivatives. This is because their price derives from the market value of another financial instrument, which is defined as underlying. For example, the underlying market is defined as investment in stocks, financial indices, currencies, interest rates, etc.

Trading Options

According to the technical jargon, the option is defined as a contract that gives the holder the right, but not the obligation to buy or sell the security on which the option is written. Obviously, everything has at a certain exercise price and by a certain date.

In short, with an option contract, you have the right but not the obligation to buy or sell an asset at a certain price and within a certain date, making the payment of the cost immediately to obtain this right. If conditions are favorable to the trader, this can confirm the purchase or sale, according to the option reported, yielding the investment.

In the opposite case, however, if the conditions are not favorable to the trader, no operation will be concluded, but the loss will be avoided, even if the initial cost paid has not been recovered. Within this basic operation, there are also several advanced strategies, such as that of selling these contracts instead of buying them.

Trading Futures

When we talk about futures contracts, this refers to a type of futures contract. In this contract, the parties undertake to exchange, on a given date, a certain quantity of certain financial assets at the set price.

In practice, when working with futures contracts, the trader obtains the right to buy or sell an asset at the price and on a fixed date, as soon as the transaction is opened. When the futures contract is resolved, the trader will be able to benefit from it and obtain an income, due to the difference between the purchase price or the selling price established with the future, and the current market price of the asset underlying the future itself.

As in everything, if the difference is positive, a profit will be realized; otherwise, a loss will occur. When we talk about futures contracts, we always refer to underlying assets of the futures. These are divided into categories:

1. *Real categories*. Such as commodities, i.e., raw materials such as wheat, gold, metals, coffee, etc.
2. *Financial categories*. Only in this case will we talk about financial futures, whose underlying assets may be, for example, a currency, currency futures, or a stock exchange index.

Trading Forex

The Forex market, which stands for Foreign Exchange Market, is the currency market, which is the largest market in the world, if not the best known in our time. Forex is not only defined as an investment tool but a real market, where it is possible to trade through different instruments, such as options or futures or, even simply, buy and sell, thanks to the spot market.

In the Forex market, only currency pairs are exchanged, and there are no other assets. Consequently, the currency that you buy or sell, you do not buy it or sell it individually, but always in pairs. Therefore, all traders and speculators trade precisely in the fact of this change, or trade on the exchange, on the fact that a currency grows and one decreases.

To make Forex trading, if, on the one hand, presupposes the possibility of bringing home a positive result, on the other hand, it assumes the risk of complete insolvency or, in other words, the total loss of capital traded.

Furthermore, trading in the Forex market also requires a fairly complete level of knowledge and experience. That's why we always recommend only regulated brokers, which, in addition to ensuring the capital of the trader, also manages to ensure adequate training of the trader.

Chapter 5
Social Trading

Social Trading can be defined as one of the best strategies, in our opinion, of online trading. Thanks to social trading, traders can share their strategies with each other, but they can also ask for advice on the type of investment.

It is not recently that we talk about social trading and copy trader, just in online trading. One of the best brokers to offer this service is eToro, a veteran and the founding father of social trading and copy trader, which allows all traders to trade by copying the best traders.

Thanks to Social Trading, the trader is the direct manager of their own money, that is, he does not entrust them to any external manager, as with the online trading platforms, he will be the owner of his own capital and will be responsible for his own investment.

At the same time, however, it is not the trader who has to buy or sell, but thanks to specialized trading platforms, the trader can view a portfolio of market participants called traders, observe them, and compare and share their strategies and style and the trader's performance. In case they are interested in this trader, they can also decide to link to his account to the chosen trader, thanks to the copy trader system.

When you copy your chosen trader, all transactions made by that trader will be photocopied directly on his personal account; in short, it will be automatically replicated on the trader's account through the Social Trading platform.

So, it will not be the trader to carry out the trading operations, but the trader that has been decided to copy that will work for us. Obviously, this will earn a percentage of our earnings, while those who trade will earn the percentage traded on that trade.

To operate with social trading, you just have to open an online trading account with eToro, choose your favorite traders, and bet on them. These will generate profits on our behalf. The trader is only responsible for diversifying the portfolio and choosing the best traders to follow.

The gains that can be obtained obviously change from trader to trader but, above all, on the basis of traded capital, as well as losses. In our opinion, we can only say that the profit percentages, for each positive trade, are higher than those of bonds and shares, as well as investment times can be shortened.

The risk associated with online trading certainly exists but, if you take the due precautions, thanks to the right knowledge, certainly can be reduced, even compared to the Forex DIY, seen and considered that the trader copied, is not a beginner trader but an expert, also confirmed by the profits he has earned.

Chapter 6
Trading and Time

When one thinks of the different investment tools, if not the practice, of the investment in general, one cannot but considers the temporal factor. This is one of the factors that other miller discourages the trader. But why?

In these times, we are so used to the concept of *everything and immediately* we cannot wait any longer. We demand everything immediately, also losing track of time and the precious value of time.

Unfortunately, in online trading, you cannot expect to have everything and immediately, but above all, we cannot expect to become experienced traders and professionals in just under a month or worse than a week.

You cannot think of becoming an expert trader if you do not want to study and practice! In online trading, but also in investment, in general, it takes time to learn how to trade. Another advice that is not feasible at the moment is to think about spending some time to find a deserving, professional, and worthy investment and investment technique.

When trading, it must be done seriously and professionally. If, for example, we trade in a trading strategy based on currency trading, with a maximum payout of 65% for a positively closed trade, then we must enter the perspective that we must give money to work with a specific strategy.

If you are following the market trend, it will be counterproductive to exit the market because, in addition to losing its capital, you may not even get the desired return. That's why time is money, and it should not be wasted unnecessarily. Above all, hurry is a bad companion.

The time factor is also one of the main factors for which it is decided better to entrust its capital to a financial expert so that this is to make the choices for them. Very often, however, this trust is not always repaid by an increase in one's capital. Most often this capital is completely lost.

The Importance of the Right Time and Timing

Understanding when the right time to trade is very important. Giving money to mature is certainly one of the most determining factors for the success of your investment. The fundamental concept remains the same: within what you want to earn money and how to earn them.

To make sure that you know, in advance, how much you can earn and how to make money for us, you cannot rely on chance, and above all, we cannot expect to waste time but not even to demand everything immediately.

Everything has its time; also in investment, they have their right times and their importance. As you can see, even the right timing serves to give way to the investment, to make your own cycle, and to express that reasonable expectation. The right setup also serves your capital to survive in any situation, resist negative moments, and always have the strength to start again.

Avoiding Risks

To better understand the risks involved in trading in risky strategies, it seems right to remember those that are the right principles. Suppose you can trade $10,000 in a strategy that is 50% risk. This strategy was put in place to double the capital within a maximum of 3. Highly risky strategy from our point of view as it could result in the total loss of the entire capital. This operation is recommended only to experienced traders.

With this example, we have made you understand how these operations allow you to double or triple the capital within a few months but also how you can lose all your capital in a matter of months. In fact, by implementing these dangerous strategies, you will also see the account halved, or entirely burned, within a few weeks.

To understand everything better, let's take another example. According to your trading strategies, you have traded on a particular asset with a strategy and think that this can give you a return of 50% within a month.

To not fall into error, we advise you to set the opposite goal or try to ask the question: how would it be if in half a month you lost half of the bill? Here is therefore explained and understood in a simple and fast way on what is the right time, but especially those that are the wrong strategies not to be adopted.

Limiting Damages of Social Trading

Many wonder if social trading is the right strategy to avoid wasting time and earning, thanks to social trading. Before proceeding, we remind you that social trading is not a risk-free form of trading, even if the risk, in this case, is reduced. To trade in social trading, we believe it is essential to operate for a period of time between 9 and 12 months minimum. This is for one simple reason. Before choosing an investment system, you must see the performance for at least a year. In this sense, there is no need to follow a trader, 24 hours a day, 365 days a year, but only that you have to consult all the data of all the operations performed during the year, perhaps with the help with special tools that simplify reading.

Once you understand how to trade, but above all, you understand how much trading and who you want to trade in, you have to consider the risk that you are willing to run. Beyond this limit, it is advisable to leave it alone.

In most cases, the conditions that have led you to make a certain investment choice must have solid foundations so that the investment can yield. That's why a period of 12 months is a period enough to make you understand if your investment is right or wrong.

Chapter 7
Trading and Commitment

Time is a tyrant, but not always! The first thing you have to concentrate on to put in place a good investment is the time you want to dedicate to the investment itself, or even to learn the new discipline with which you want to operate.

Our advice is to take all the time necessary to study the new techniques, to implement the new strategies, and to metabolize all the concepts well. Only after you have done this, we advise you to start trading in the stock market or trading with an online demo account.

Even if your investment objective is different from online trading, there's no problem. The important thing is to continue and persist in your own way to achieve the precise objective.

Have a Clear Goal

Another point on which we will focus is the investment objective. This point is very important for the trader and for his success also based on what is the psychology of an individual.

However, knowing how to do it is not a foregone conclusion. This presupposes a good capacity for analysis. In fact, in the investment, there is only the objective to be achieved; there is nothing but the possibility of victory and the possibility of losses and risks.

1)   Be the owner of your own money.

Being owners of their own money presupposes the possibility of being aware of recognizing one's own limits, having a precise objective and above all having the theoretical foundations to achieve it. In this sense, we must put ourselves in the advantageous condition of knowing which risks we can run. Recognizing them is really the starting point for a good investment. It would not make sense to start a new investment if you do not know the limits and do not know what the risks related to it are.

2)   Know yourself.

Once the first point has been made, and the objective is clear but also the risk related to the loss of one's own money, one has to do is start analyzing oneself. In this way, we can understand whether it is worthwhile trading with long-term strategies or short-term strategies, whether it is better to trade a certain capital rather than another, or better diversify investment objectives. It is better not to make fun of yourself if you do not want to lose your capital completely, you must recognize your limits, predict any reactions, and risk tolerance levels.

To better understand, let's take a practical example. Suppose we have two investment strategies. In both cases, the aim is to achieve 50% increase in initial capital. Based on what is in the first statistic, you can get a profit of 50% over a year, risking half the capital. According to the second strategy, on the other hand, we will obtain a profit of 50% over 2 years, but in a maximum period of 24 months, risking only 20% of the capital. At this point, a question arises: what kind of strategy to use? In the first case, it is true that the goal is reached first, but it is also true that the percentages in case of loss are greater. If you come to check a negative period of time, even just three months, it is not easy not to consider it as a problem. Without making fun of it, nobody likes losing, and losing half of their capital can be a real blow to everyone.

But there is also the positive side; after the black period of three months, one could follow with half of the remaining capital and could concentrate on the remaining months to complete its strategy and make a profit. Once the negative moment has passed, the strategy begins to grind very good operations, and in the following 9 months, the account recovers not only the losses but closes positively with a further increase. Now, this we have proposed to you is just one example. Not all traders close their accounts in a year. So, pay close attention. In the second case, however, the strategy can be used by all those who prefer to operate more safely and that we recommend because it limits the risk even if the waiting time is greater.

3) Objective = Earnings; Objective = Risk

Another important point to keep in mind and that must always be considered is what you want to earn, but above all, we are willing to risk to get that profit. Many times, it is more useful to rely on instinct and not on rationality, but this method does not always work. In this sense, we want to understand that it is much more prudent to evaluate the situation in which we find ourselves from time to time, to prefix the objectives we want to achieve at a given moment, and the possibility we have of reaching that goal. Therefore, knowing oneself before starting an investment is an excellent strategy to understand even the real goals and the real risks we can bear.

Chapter 8
Compound Interest

Compound interest is one of the most powerful tools at your disposal, so study it carefully. It is an interest that is not collected but is added to the initial capital that generated it to be traded again.

This means that for the period following the one that generated the interest, interests will be traded and accrued not only on the initial capital but also on the interest accrued in the first period.

In a subsequent period, the discussion does not change; the interest will always accrue on the initial capital, to whose capital are added also the interest accrued in the first period and the interest accrued in the second period (which, in turn, have accrued on the interests of the former).

How to Calculate Compound Interests

Suppose you have the opportunity to trade with an initial capital of $10,000. In this case, you will choose an investment plan that can guarantee a minimum return of 10% per annum for 5 years. During the first year, you decide to take the accrued interest out of the investment.

At this point, after the first 5 years of investment, you will have collected $1000 per year for 5 years which, together with the initial capital, make a total of $15,000. If, on the other hand, it is decided to trade the interests again, exploiting the compound interest system, you will have, at the end of the 5 years, the total capital of $16,105.10.

If the entire capital is redeemed again for another 5 years, you will have a total capital of $20,000, using the first strategy, while reinvesting the interest could also reach the figure of $25,937.42.

Trade Today With Compound Interests

Compound interests need a long enough time to function better. In fact, time is a fundamental factor for them. Patience and just time are two very important factors to allow the interests to mature significantly on themselves. We can also consider trading on compound interest with social trading. The investment process will be the same, for most transactions, based on what is the investment capital.

Assuming we obtain a monthly return of 5%, we also decide to trade the interests, trading and increasing in this way the weight of the transactions that will be replicated. So, based on what has been stated so far, we can tell you that time works for you and that the more you learn how to use it, the more it pays off.

Now, the first thing to do is to understand that compounded interests are also a form of investment and that compound interests are an excellent tool for increasing capital.

If you think, then, that if you have a modest capital or you have a capital to trade, and you hope to get exaggerated interests, then you really are completely out of the way.

Chapter 9
Investing in Yourself

As I have already said and repeatedly stated, trading does not mean betting, let alone gambling. Trading means being based on precise studies and statistics. This is the only method that allows you to find reasonable expectations of success to also exploit a specific strategy.

The greater your studies will be, the more strategies will be learned, the lower the chances of running into mistakes, the greater the returns will be, and the lower the risks of losing one's capital.

The greater the time to devote to study and to learning, the greater the successes that can be achieved. However, there is also the risk of studying and applying a lot. The risk cannot be canceled; at most, it can be reduced.

Unfortunately, all investments are based essentially on people and their decisions. There is no investment for everyone, and there is no equal strategy for everyone. There are many strategies for many traders, not mathematical laws.

Fear and greed are the two emotions that must be controlled if you want to succeed in the right investment. Both these emotions move the markets. Although they are two human conditions that can be studied and analyzed, they can never be translated into perfect mathematical laws.

Even if you trade with a strategy that allows you to close in profit more than 90% of the time, 10% represents the risk and must not be put aside but must always be considered. This happens very often to traders or investors who do not want to close the operations at a loss or do not want to abandon the wrong investment admitting the mistake because they believe that sooner or later they will return in their favor.

Chapter 10
Should You Challenge the Market?

One of the fundamental strategies for not losing the entire capital is to consider the risk related to market movements but, above all, to never challenge the market and go against the trend.

Trading in the stock market is not easy; even the strategy of the best traders can turn out to be a failure if you insist on challenging the market. Never think about this but, above all, never consider a movement of the market equal to the other. So, you never have to think about being able to beat the market ahead of time.

It is advisable not to challenge the market but, above all, to keep in mind that the market is always right. If you want to trade in serious and professional ways, you have to study, set a strategy, and follow it both positively and negatively if the initial conditions are always the same.

In the case instead of changing the starting conditions, we suggest to evaluate everything with a cold mind and evaluate whether it is still appropriate to continue on that road or change the road. This means accepting the error, but it is always better to understand the mistake of losing the entire capital.

Chapter 11
Portfolios and Diversification

The best money protection strategy is portfolio diversification. The investment portfolio is certainly one of the terms the traders feel most when it comes to investment. But what is the portfolio?

The investment portfolio can be understood as a combination of suitably combined financial assets to achieve the objective. In other words, it represents the set of all financial products or strategies on which you have decided to trade.

Advantages of the Diversified Portfolio

So, diversifying your portfolio is crucial to gain and suffer the effects of losses as little as possible. In fact, the goal of the trader is to earn in the long term and not in the short term.

Therefore, the best strategy is to diversify the portfolio and to unite different types of instruments that operate in different ways to reduce the overall risk of the investment itself. We can also consider that investments, with a diversification of the portfolio, are statistically less than a little or no diversified at all.

If the trader decides to trade in stocks and bonds by diversifying his portfolio, then we can consider different hypotheses. We can, therefore, consider bonds as safer instruments than stocks. In this case, the trader who wants a conservative portfolio, or trading with a low risk, we recommend trading two-thirds of his capital per bond, while a small part allocates it to the shares. If, on the other hand, you prefer a more aggressive approach, or a higher profit, based on the level of risk you are willing to run, then it is preferable to trade at least two-thirds of your capital to the shares and the remainder to bonds and funds.

Trading With Government Bonds: Right or Wrong?

For those who want to trade in bonds, or even for those who want to trade in much safer sectors, even if less profitable, we recommend government bonds. Taking into consideration the government bonds, we can see how these are divided into different categories based on what is the degree of security and return.

To trade with government bonds, the rating agencies are used as Standard & Poor's, Moody's and Fitch, and the Rate, i.e., the votes, AAA, AA +, etc. By diversifying the portfolio with government bonds, it will be possible to trade two-thirds in bonds or 65% in government bonds or sovereign national institutions, but which have a rating of AAA or AA +, while the remainder allocates it to instruments bonds with lower rating ratings and more remunerative coupon rates.

The same strategy could be used for stocks. Using a more conservative approach, you can choose solid company shares that generate income over the long term. Trading the entire capital on a single Signal Provider is not the best solution, and we never recommend it. Obviously, attention is used to distinguish the parameters with which we analyze the performance of a trader, thanks to which it is possible to distinguish the conservative Signal Providers from the more aggressive ones.

Finally, we remind you never to exaggerate even in the diversification of the portfolio. Diversifying the portfolio excessively is not the right strategy, but above all, it is not suitable for beginners.

Conclusion

Thank you for making it through to the end of *Stock Trading*, let's hope it was informative and provides you with all of the tools you need to achieve your goals whatever they may be.

The next step is to start applying what you have learned during this book and get started right away. Our suggestion is always to open up a demo account and make a few tries, before putting real money into it. Remember that you should never risk more than what you can afford to lose, so manage your capital wisely and take out profits regularly.

Finally, if you found this book useful in any way, a review on Amazon is always appreciated!

Did you know that a large percent of people who make a lot of money lose it within the first couple years?

It doesn't take much for a person to lose all of their money. Around 2 in 3 lottery winners lose all of their winnings within 5 years. If someone could lose hundreds of millions of dollars over a couple years, how fast will you lose your millions that you could make from this book?

Over the past couple years I have stumbled upon the key secret behind managing money and KEEPING it. If you follow the link below you will uncover the truth behind managing and keeping the money you make

>>> Click/Tap here to Learn the Secret Behind Money Management
<<<
Or Go to https://secretstomoneymanagement.gr8.com/

Description

Are you looking for a great book about trading stocks but every single time you purchase a course it seems that nothing makes sense? Are you scared when you hear words like "trendline," "bonds," and "futures"?

Then, this is the right book for you! In *Stock Trading*, you are going to learn everything there is to know about this topic and get insightful tips that will transform your mindset when it comes to money.

During this in-depth manual, you are going to learn about fundamental topics such as the following:

- What initial capital is required to start so that you know if you have the right credentials to get started in this amazing world or if it is time to save money before going on the attack
- What big boys do to stay ahead of the competition and get the best deals, making money even when stocks are falling
- What social trading is and how you can benefit from it
- What trading is not and how you can avoid the main mistakes of beginners
- How to time the market correctly and get the most out of your trades
- A lot of hidden information that will boost your education and get you started investing as fast as possible

As you can see, this book is full of details and goes very deep on the subject. Prior experience is not required, and the manual was written especially for those who do not know anything about investing.

If you have been on the fence for a while and want to take your investing game to the next level, this is the right book for you. Get it now at a special price and act fast; it won't be so cheap forever.

www.ingramcontent.com/pod-product-compliance
Lightning Source LLC
Chambersburg PA
CBHW070504220526
45467CB00002B/557